Lavender growing on the star
A ball of purple that used to be called
Mars
Infinite rings around Saturn, made by
giants
If all of them collapsed would it be
quiet?

Thoughts so pure the sky turns white
The sun, in his infinite light,
he turns black and falls without life
Falls as if he got consumed by blight

Endlessly he descends into nothing, or
into madness
The rest of the planets get consumed
by sadness
This plague, thought she is clever
As all seem to perish, there is a hope,
the night is forever

Better you than me
That's how I want it to be
Rather have you cry on the floor
Than me banging my head on the door
I'll have you cut your wrists before I open my chest
Inside my rib cage, clockwork overused, put to the test
Can't sleep and I'm desperate after rest
Please not please me anymore
Your words exit your mouth but collapse on the floor
Yet this isn't all, I got something else in store
Yeah, yeah, pain.. I always got more

Burning blinding star
I would love you hard
My heart is made out of stone
So I just gotta love you cold

On the island of find thyself
I find endless me's that I never felt
Guess they died, bet
Made the wrong step
And I couldn't feel less

This means I'm the best of me
Whatever best that might be
And I thank myself for being true
To everything I said I was gonna do

At this rate I just don't care
Everybody is breaking their neck
To see me in action, to see me in horror
What an honor

Concept of feelings, I don't understand
Those feelings, are they like lead?
I'm good at serving that, so I take the blame
If I hurt you till now, welp, then this is the
end

Why does my happiness look like you
Is this a dream or is it true
Beams of light coming thru your chest
lighting up the room

But I'm still afraid with all this light
What if you decide to turn to night
I'll be here blind

Crying red
Laughing at my own jokes
Breaking my own bones
So the pain sends me to bed

I'm too afraid to try and be alone
Too scared to have hope

Undisclosed
My mind is stone my heart is bone

And with all my love I tell you to run
But you don't wanna trip and fall
So you suffer
With me in the same locker

I'm saying that games are fun but this is torture
You look at me with big eyes scared and uncertain
And I'm telling you over and over to run, escape
what I can't
Still here.. suffering all you can

Believe in me darling
World is just a drawing
Yet I'm tearing at it so please just exit the image
It pains me to not be able to stop this damage

My words go thru you like you are just a ghost
And I fear that my demons are making it worse
This reality is just breaking for me
Now the only thing I hope is that end is nearing

I don't really mind
Call me by whatever hate you
wanna find
Please do, I can take it all night
Call me whatever, whenever, till
you go blind

Grind me slowly to dust
Put me under rain so I rust
Can't take me down, even if you
cut my legs
I'll stand on my hands

Smiling while you cut me open
Do your worst I'm dormant
You don't know pain like me
So do your worse baby
I'm ready

Let me taste the rain
While the excess goes down the drain
Let me feel the lighting in my fingers
The power inside I let it linger

But don't trust my words for what I might say
They calculate that lighting won't strike my way
And I'm here waiting, calling it down on me
Afraid, he won't let me be

Little by little, teasing
Little by little, air is freezing
Then it strikes

Just bright
Just Might.
I'm still here
With all this power only demanding sacrifice a tear

With a bang of flashing light
A flash of white
All the dust in the universe falls on you
Of colors of red and blue
Only you could pull it thru

And all the anomalies
That take place in life seem to follow us around
They change perspective but my perspective of
you is impenetrable, sound
And I feel no pain when they kick me while I'm
downed

Memories of you flood my mind like rivers
flood villages
With a sweet touch of nostalgia and a torture
of images
Yet all the screams I hear in my head are not
mine
And all the pain in my heart took more than
just your time
Guess I was worth a dime..
But you never meant to pay

From a dead sea
To a worse reality
All the meteorites are attracted to me
This universe won't let me be

I call myself ruins
But my words are ignored and,
I get overwhelmed by bandits
They want the treasure but it's all gone,
only I stand

Alone I stand, like a cactus in the desert
Like a piece of wood, drifting on the sea
Alone in this blizzard
Alone, always just me

Let us exist in a world without life
Nothing stops it from doing it right
Nothing might..
Trick us into making a mistake
Their plans go in the oven but don't bake

Everything is at hand
But fear not, I have aces in my sleeve
Life is a roulette I believe
And I cheat , I'm contraband

Can't bare being fair
They don't play by the rules so I go in solo as a pair
I'll be searched for until I'm dead
So guess they'll search forever this wicked land
Leaving Hell over and over again as contraband

Magic
Tragic
Abracadabra, make it static
Mind start roaming for your image

It can't find it, now he sad
He starts going down bad
Only wanting to die, lamb for slaughter
Burn in hell, hotter and hotter

His eyes become rivers, traumatized
From tears to blood, comatized
Going down in the ice filled tub, one last time
With his last strength he says bye

They can't replace you
My heart still cold and blue
They try endlessly to please me
But nothing ever comes to be

You rained my metal heart and now its all rust
My brain might bust
All the pipes are overloading
And I feel my frustrating flowing

I hate myself because it lacks you
All good in me was you and only you
Now it's just madness
Slowly being replaced by emptiness

Lung almost gone, it drags me on the way
I am chained in a maiden, all I have to say
There is no God helping me out
And if there is one speaking, you need to speak a
lil more loud

Done wrong, can't deny the past
Can forgive but can't forget what still has wrath
But I'll never forgive either, I'll live with a grudge
Nothing can change that, I won't budge

He isn't moving fast, he takes his time
My lung is slow to take me home
I'm going to Hell, all is fine
Destiny said I had to crumble like Rome

I'm searching,
I'm searching
For what it feels like,
eternity

Roaming endless possibilities
All with the same ending
I hate this disability
To finally die and stop hating

When the soil rots and my bones still drag on
When they say "I love you" and everything starts
to be gone
With a sweet whisper never said meaning
goodbye
When they jump off cliffs with the purpose to die

Not wanting to see my suffering
No desire in keeping me close
They'll rather die..
Than love me for a second more

Fermenting air
Despair
Dogs crying, crawling without legs
Brimstone covering the clouds
We can't hear them, even when they are loud

Robotized, lobotomized
Separated from their eyes
Cut from the source, what a surprise
Waking up not owning control
Fearing to be stoned

Corrupted from the core
Dehumanized
Destruction of this planet..
or
An unnecessary sacrifice

You promised me flowers of undying love
But they decayed into compost and I had it
thrown
You promise to take stars and make me a crown
But all of it was just words searching around

Said with glowing eyes that your world is me
But when I knocked at your door it was occupied
Thought it was a nightmare, I was terrified
But then I didn't wake up, it was certified

With undying love I told you, why is it so
Undying, because there is no more to die for
All of it died, like a star being absorbed by the
universe
All of it cried, like a petal being removed from the
rest of the rose

Oh, it's you
Your glow has changed
Smile faded away
All of him couldn't be swayed?
Now I'm next in line, replace?
But when I gave you millions, you looked for
better place

I was a star dying, waiting to be reborn
You were my flame, promising me a home
Then you disappeared, vanished
Found you millions of years away, being
tarnished

I would've offered help, but you chose this way
I would've gave you me, but you didn't want to
stay
Guess... I was just display

In heart, apocalypse
Slowly filling with hate
All of it man made
With evil intent

Why help when you fall harder
When they don't feel your stutter
And all their words are robotic
No care, you are just static

On their frequencies
You are an anomaly
Stop trying...
Give up being good..
Yeah.. you should

Feeding trust with a spoon
I know baby that I act as a buffoon
Doing it for you
I'm loosening the noose

Wanting too much, too fast
You got confused why I even asked
I guess I'm a nympho for the info
Wanted to surprise you but I didn't hit the bingo

But we aren't there yet, I got it
Still small, I couldn't fit
The keyhole is there, but so is the door
So I guess I'll hope you gon' open it for..
me

Lighting breaking the sky in two
Face to face, me and you
He will make you cry, he'll do
I can't stop it, I'm forced watching it play thru

My lips are blue, lungs are covered in water
Bubbles raise thru my eyes, my hands get harder
I sink like a sack of stones
Fearing everything he has done

When he takes control over me
He'll cut you up, no empathy
Fearing loss, but more importantly
Losing you entirely

Rhythm of the screams

They touch lightly the world I am in, but nothing is what it seems
I'm left tied to my bed, but it was a dream
Then I wake up in a reality that is a loop of asking "what I could've been"

With no purpose but to inflict pain on itself
With nothing going on but to burn in Hell
I challenge all the demons that haunt me
Come get my soul
I'm ready for you all

And I challenge my brain, because you separated from me
If you want me to die, so be it
Kill me yourself, don't make me die from an image
Don't kill me using that weak tactic of never sleeping
Just pull yourself from my system, cut yourself
We both die, not just myself

Stab stab stab, we go at it again
"We are over it", nope, we are not
I'll hate your guts till my guts rot
If I have to feed you I'll feed you pain

Tonight, Tonight, chances of rain
So be sure to prepare the brain
Some stillness is in the air
And it can make you go insane

I'm brave Dad, let me play in the storm
No son no, you might get blown
Lighting striking the scenery, makes you cower
What point of being a king when you are stuck in
your own tower

No signal, we don't connect
It doesn't go thru
Screen blue
I scream too

My words don't concentrate enough
My eyes lose sight
I fear I might
Break the cuff

We are not that type of people
We don't want the glory
We are not that type of people
We only want the money

There is no glory in death
So we keep on living
There is no hope in tomorrow
If you don't get to see it

And believe me
When I say
We are not the same
I want more and more every single day
Won't ever stop

Remember the remembering
But who cares
They are just dirt in ground without any memory
They just play for time, long gone
Bone.

Room inside their rib cage
Finding a home, old age
We might speak the same thing but I'm on a different page
I'm trying to say something, you think you get it, you don't,
stage

And look at me dance with make up on, on applause, on
pause
I smile in the mirror but it doesn't smile back
I only want it to die, my mind
My echo to stop running down the halls

Because this is torture, but doesn't bother you
I am tied to the chair, oh what do I do
Slowly my skin removed, straight to my soul
WHY NOT TAKE IT ALL

Sleepless nights of terror, thanks to myself
I made the worst, in hell
And I look bad, need help
But all is swiped under the rug.
Put on repeat,
repeat

We walking but it seems so backwards
Grab the records
How many love you, blah, blah, whatever
We change like we are weather

But baby you got me like a fever
I'm sick, eating my nails like a beaver
You make me wanna cry, river
But I wanna be brave, gonna stop the shiver

Not cold no, I burn with you in my heart
And when I look at you I see art
Guess we hate each other, we do our part
But in the end.. we come back

Losing myself in my own mind
He is there, the hive
Oh and I'm fighting all alone, I'm brave
Yet I am losing the fight and I feel treated like a
slave

Cuz nothing I say matters, ever
And what I say falls like rain, weather
They told me to go and talk with Heather
But I don't like so, whatever

They can't understand that I don't need no one
That I can just spend eternity in my mind
Composing myself nice, fighting the mirror
If he ever gets out this planet will get Minor

Crying my soul in this darkness of a room
Absorbing madness in this void of a state
Is this my fate?
Can I switch it up if I present my head some
boom?

And I lose myself in you
All the worlds that I go to
They are nothing without your face
They are nothing without your grace

Like the moon in the sky, you offer me light
in this darkness of a time
And if you were to collapse, I would turn into
Atlas and hold you higher

Always

Soul divided
Throw all my conscious in Hell
Sorrow consume me well
All I ever wanted was help

And I reached for angels but they slapped
my hand
I tried for Heaven but it was occupied
Losing pieces of my mind
Losing body parts in a different land

I'll burn my life
I'll burn it alive

Feeling lost at sea like a sailor without a ship
I'm losing myself in your eyes, my words can't
find the exit

And I wish I knew why
And I wish I could say Hi
I'm shy, shelled, I need help
But I won't ask for it, not even if I go to Hell

Walking away from paradise because the fear
got over
Refuse is imminent, I'll get destroyed, can't
stay sober
Then I'll drink myself into death, so she
touches my lips
She wants me to come with her, I follow her
hips

Taking me far away from existence, in a place
without of time
So I can spend eternity wishing you were
mine

Stone of betrayal, thrown towards
All my glass bones
They went into my home
And found all my wands

I tried to give little bits of magic
Now they want to end me, tragic
But I'm leaving
With my strong believing

That I can be more by having hope in myself
I don't feel the need to beg
If there is mercy, why burn me at stake?
If there is saving, why don't hands fill the holes in
my neck?

I'm speechless

I'm behaving
So stop pretending
That I'm the only one
I know I'm not

You don't have to lie again
I know you've been sent by a friend
You had to check on me, monitor my pulse
If you only knew I'm both deaf and mute

I don't hear your words and neither say them
back
You might not completely understand
I'm blind to your words, to what you want to
paint
So just leave me and don't come again
You weren't here on your own

I'm right behind you small human
Gently you swim in my ocean
In all the abyss that is my home
You are afraid.. your heart is beating strong

Against the will of the waves
You swim away from me wanting to scream
But you can't
And I'm faster

I touch your feet with the top of my head
You push your fingers in my eyes
My only wish was to be friends
Now my wish is for your life to end.

You are stuck in my home
There's nothing you can get done
The night is long..
And I have plans for Us.

Sin after sin
Father let me see
How I still swim without a fin
And how do I drown while heaving gills

I gave you all I got
I gave you all I didn't have
You still threw me in hell
And I screamed your name in vain

I'm taking you down with me
If I am deemed a traitor then let it be
Tired pretending your choices are good
Tired of acting under your name, behind your hood
No strength, can't fight me, otherwise you would

Roaming blind in a world of thorns
Even got back my horns
They are setting the stones
So I give them bones

Hear my boss calling, he is very thrilled
That I got back in the attic, he is offering me
a deal
Return as his hand, serve the Hell again
I want to.. but what would she say

My eyes are still there, searching for me
I am terrified what I might turn up to be
Into Hell I want to plunge..
But while she is still here, I won't budge

High kicks
With low impact
I can hear my heart,
it just doesn't want any of this crap

Just let me go
I don't belong
Don't feel at home
Let me fly away from this steel dome

Breaking doors
Scratching walls
Let me the fuck out
I talk loud

Chained to bad
Death follows
All their souls are hollow
I am going mad

Can't slip away
There is no future I can see
Day by day
I need death to escape, but they won't let me

Lacking everything that makes me human
Trying to find something that makes me feel
My emotions, they have one ruler
And they are forced of being cruel

Punishing my whole existence
While I just want to be left alone
I know it's all my fault..
But I didn't wish I was born

Stars aligned, drank too much wine
And I cry, they are so vile
I am too small, in a big body
They all know me, yet I am nobody

Looking at sky
Is anything there? why hide?
Oh and so much I wish I could fly
To see if there is any Light

Could it truly be a longer than the end?
Will the soul break or only bend?
If it breaks, can it mend?
Or at the finish, you just end up dead

Will I walk streets of gold?
Or in the fire I would feel burned but cold?
Maybe there isn't anything at all..
Just the fear of fall

Breath of death giving life
Only if wrong could be so right
In the end to see despair on sight
And to point at its growing fright

To see how fast you can turn around
To hear what's their last sound
Holding their hand, will they trade your place?
Will they give their soul to live as empty as a shoe lace?

Can anybody grow in their last despair?
Will anybody forgive what is to forget?
Not all will end in Heaven, and that is fair
But believe it when I say we all start in Hell

Speaking low about myself, so I think it's true
I am high enough to be too good for you
Whenever you want to talk, ask the hand
In front of me you crawl, don't stand

So high I touch the sky
Stars tickling my fingers
There is.. a glow in my eyes
But I shouldn't linger

Got greatness to achieve
Renown to be made
Had enough to grieve
Time for me to become legend and never fade

This suffering eats thru me
And I wish I could be
Someone happy

Wishing I could say I am good..
But I am always on the redemption road
It feels like I'll forever walk alone

Trapped inside this loop of paying sins with good
dealings
I wish I knew my true feelings
Something inside stops me from being..
Good

I don't know how love feels, if it's
cold or if it burns
I keep giving it but there are no
returns
Wish I would know, truly
And I have this feeling that I'm
about to blow, surely

My heart is like a c4, explosive
But it has more rust on it than
metal, corrosive
Believe me when I say that I'm on
my last leg
I am literally crawling to the end

I keep burning harder and harder
IF YOU ARE IN HEAVEN CAN YOU SEE ME FATHER?
I am engulfed in flames to grab me to Hell
When I reach it I'll say you kept me well

Kept me from being happy
Gave me this growing hate
And it was eating my booones
Was this my true fate?

Sitting corrupted with a mind of stone in a circle of
flowers
I wish I could say that I end well but I will be frozen
in my house um..
In the end I did and will do what others before me did
Doing nothing else but continuing the legacy

Isn't it lovely?
Burning yourself once more
Reduced to nothing but bone
Crying you can find none

Trying to reach the light
But it was from an angler
You get swallowed without a fight
Inside you that guy tries to escape, the
strangler

But you can't just cut him out
Neither can you keep him forever
This jail is breaking, bone after bone
No, it doesn't get better

I don't get past the door
Not anymore
Sleeping on the mat, knocking
But why? Why keep trying?

It's a meaningless search of feeling good
No, I'm not in the mood
Not feeling like someone else tonight
So take a second and take it right..

I hate what this all is
Just biz
There is nothing working for us
So one should take the bus
Away

Stop
Think a second
Redirect your intention
Not the one you should try
I am lost in abyss so don't cry
Can't see myself in the mirror
I want to break it and die of cold in a river

My reflection is me
And I don't like it
Seeing the truth smile
I wish I was blind

Ending up frozen in complete
nothingness
All my problems are gonna celebrate in a
bone dress
They will parade my dead corpse in hell
There is no stopping me from enjoying
being dead

When all you've done is broken
Never correct, should've never opened..
Should've ended it sooner
But I couldn't

The nights are white,
the days are black
I wish it would all turn back
To the good days that might..

Might give me something good
Get me out of this mood
If you can put a smile on me you should
It might be the last time you could..

This words are for display
I use them every single day
Don't believe anything I say
You never know the evil they may..

Black sweat falling
Snow melting
Me smiling
With a hidden amount of hatred

You never know the inside
All the problems that I hide
Nobody can help so I just ride
I'm on my way to Hell tonight

Look at me and say
"Your soul is poor"
But it has more depth than the ocean floor
Only that I hide it because it's all wrong

And I wish I could write between tears
And I wish I knew how to hide my fears
And I really wish I knew how to feel good
I.. really should

But I am sorry a million times more for
cutting it short
I wish I could tell you my soul's worth
Yet I can't sell it because nobody is buying
Guess not even death cares about me
dying

A pact made with self to find peace
In times of war when you can't find ease
With nights of terror going down your
spine
You never know if your end will feel
right

That feeling of unknown is the greatest
fear
And I would die right now if I knew the
deal
But I'm afraid of what is there.. no
I am afraid of nothing being there at all

Death doesn't seem so bad when it starts
something new
But we don't know for certain it does so
we live with plenty and end with few
And I am really afraid of it all..
Afraid of not being able to exist.. not
"here".. but anymore

Everything is so cold
Can't even find my coal
Inside.. it must reside

Alleys of empty, filled with people
To you sweetheart, there is no equal
And it's eating me thru

This anger, this loneliness..
Haunted by what it could've been
And I wish I could love you as you need

I'm truly sorry
Forever lost searching inside my body
Searching for good...

New year new me new you
New everything that didn't have the luck to
pass thru
I know it's a torture being alive, but you gotta
work it
There is a day where all will be worth it

It might take you just a little long'
Might make you wish you stop
And I.. believe that all have their role
Every single tear you drop

Even if you feel like salt in rain
One day, you will want to feel pain
Every emotion you have now.. it will be gone
You'll enter a new world

A new everything..

Caught, eclipse
Happiness in a jar
Living by the moment
Hearing it again, remembering it all

That cut done with a sugar knife
A tear made by feeling so good.. it's bad
That moment of "what I was"
Followed by what you are

That sad little truth that once was better
That moment you realize you might never
get another
Quiet after screaming for your life
But your life is deaf, blind
It's killing

Searching without luck
Running out of rabbit feet
And I feel lighting has struck
And I fear that I wasn't there to greet

I'm running out of time
Feeling like that for a long while
Wasn't completely sure
Why my heart has stopped and my fingers
were blue

In the end I managed to find out
Why Death was always above me in a cloud
She was hiding, she didn't want to say
That I died and it's time to go another way
The only way

All my life
I've been ready all this time
Payed in blood the full price
Played it lucky I rolled the dice

And Death I love you
Coming all this way dressed in black and blue
I know it's you, there is no need to say no
The only thing I wished to feel is what I'm feeling
now
Death you give one last wish
And my last wish was to feel love
Even if lasts seconds, I'll treasure it forever
In Hell for eternity I'll still remember
Chained to a rock above lava, screams of terror
blowing my mind
I would forever remember you giving me my first
time

Death your lips feel so cold in their warmth
Your voice is so sweet while it cuts
Eyes calm me while I die on the floor
There is no way of me knowing what I'm dying from
But it's good.. you are good..
I love you too

Buried above ground
So flowers can grow on my lifeless corpse
Even in death there is life
That is how it goes

On my crimson veins, they get drawn
In my bones, they get warm
Untouched, I live on
In the petals that grow

A little piece of me, that dies and comes back
I wither in the winter, bloom in spring
And I love it when the birds sing
I will forever live

Road of ash
Road to the gate
Am I on the right path?
Because.. I want life, and this leads to death

I am grasping for air inside myself
Trying to tell everything is right
Is it now? I might die tonight
Strange.. what I felt

Just like touching ice, but with your whole body
Just feeling alive.. but your life escaping sadly
You want it back.. yet it just slips thru your
fingers
You shed a tear, but you shouldn't linger
The gate is open

Cry of don't do it now
Don't hang me
But they will and so it will be
That the hanged man will suffer eternity
That he will return endlessly
To life

And his return is just to die minutes later
So it has been spoken by the ancient
That one has to suffer for all
It isn't fair
Yet nobody cares

For that they are happy..
Happy they aren't in his place

No surprises
No surprises
When the sun rises

I want no "I have something for you"
Because I don't want nothing from you
Not trying to be rude
Not that I would care I come out as a brute

Don't really care where you going
Don't care if you don't say goodbye
I won't probably be there to hear them.. or alive

Running out of sand and my mistress is calling
And I've been stalling
But for how long with all the sand fell
How long till the end

Everything that goes around
Comes around then dies, it is bound
Little creatures with no hope for the future
This planet is gonna die and there is no feature

I might be the reason but I don't know
The inside of me is chaotic and I wish I could float
Float straight in the sun, die in a second
For every moment I live the planet is in danger, I reckon

Inside Hell they run away from me
From my anger, from my hatred, from everything I can be..
Destruction was an inside joke, I'm taking it outside
I see flames, death, but I can't see my mind

Severe,
trauma
Left,
the sauna
Entered,
the fridge
Unhinged

On the edge of the knife
I feel chainsaws dancing, they feel light
So I might take them for a test drive

You are making a lot of sense when you sip tea from
you cup
And I have a lot of plans for those like you without a
doubt
Cuz baby I'm no farmer but thru you I would plow
I just want to see blood dripping from you, don't care
how

If I have to give you 50 new holes, so be it
Told you I am Hell, you wouldn't believe it
On the edge of breaking my humanity.. I know for
sure
That once I hit it I can never return..

Roaming blind in a world of thorns
Even got back my horns
They are setting the stones
So I give them bones

Hear my boss calling, he is very thrilled
That I got back in the attic, he is offering me a deal
Return as his hand, serve the Hell again
I want to.. but what would she say

My eyes are still there, searching for me
I am terrified what I might turn up to be
Into Hell I want to plunge..
But while she is still here, I won't budge

Following 22 lines of madness
Complete darkness
Illuminated mind as long as you got matches
If she burns in hell why wear a dress?
Filled with stress
Reluctant to speak out, my mind is a mess
I might spill my beans if you manage to press
Either that or my cheek you can caress
For secrets, the level of dirt I let you guess
And my love I have to confess
I gave Satan your address
In his way of speaking there was a finesse
My love for you couldn't fight, he took the success
Eternal looking for more progress
His army of darkness rises against the angels oppress
To all my secrets he has access
My tries are futile, he makes me depress
Trying too hard to impress
Guilt was eating me alive so I had to redress..
I wasn't totally innocent.. well, even less
Guilty, but I couldn't express..
Hope you can forgive me, I can't, self repress
If you don't, I'll understand, demons don't deserve forgiveness

See no evil
In my sky eyes
In my weird smile
In my clear face

Hear no evil
When my voice starts to work
My words try to find a home
In your heart, your soul, your world

Seek no evil
In me anymore
You'll end up breaking down the door
To escape my Hell

Words wasted on souls left behind
I reach a new state of mind
I am a new mine
With all due respect I just don't care
You are just side characters in my main story
Just acolytes
If you could only see this lights
My eyes bleed more than one shade of red
You should've touched the sheets on the bed
Millions of sorrows they ate
From my eyes dancing down my cheek
Some just jumped in defeat
If only walls could speak what mine would say
How much would one pay
To hear the screams of torment outside my mind
The ones inside are too dangerous to try and find

Day after day
Night after night
On your steps I pray
Praying you might

Just show a finger to lift the curse
So I no longer cry in pain
No longer will I get cut in the rain
So I finally live as one may

But your temple might be false
How much hope should I have
I gave you everything I had
And you.. you never gave anything back

I'm leaving today for tomorrow
Maybe she can cure my sorrow

I'm leaving life for the after
Maybe that way I get them to gather

Leaving when I hit three with two zeroes
Leaving when I see no more heroes

And I'm leaving all that I call myself, behind
So I'm leaving this life tonight, hoping a
better one I can find

I threw my soul away
You threw me the next day
I poured myself into hands that didn't care
Didn't see it coming now I can't bear

Trying to not break and explode
All this sadness doesn't stop to flood
My heart is drowning in tar
Huh, I didn't expect to get this far

It feels like I just started being good
Now Hell calls me by name
I'm sad, it's framed
Forever

A world of madness filling people with sleep
Anger coming right after grief
Questions of why that never get an answer
Even if they have one nobody will bother

Tired people walking with their heads down
Sad people with no dreams in their grasp
They just walk, sipping from their flasks
Some "forget me later" juice to keep them away from
meltdown

Just dolls who flatten their aspirations because
somebody told them so
Children that never grow old because they were born so
A world of madness that keeps conquering
A world of madness to die in

Diagnosed with low esteem
When I think what we could've been
But it's all far away, just like a dream

Splinters of old, inside
They hurt light
But it's so often I want to die

Eyes that call, outside
Voice that keeps us warm, inside
Diagnosed with a splitter mind

All my split thoughts have a little bit of you in sight
Either you the focus or the side.. you might
Make me whole.. or strike..
Dark in my last light

Tired of your faces, all washing away
Tired of forgetting places, that I was knew
Feeling of dread, filling my insides
I wish I dead.. everybody wants to close my eyes

They fight me, but find it hard
That my nature.. can get me so mad

I'm feeling deep in cold water, bubbles washing my wounds
They are deep in trouble, surrounded by dunes
Maybe now they know it's helpless to fight the sea
Maybe now they'll be able to see..
How I feel

An ocean soon to eat the land
A man that can't control his own hand
Nightmare.. running him down long halls
Ending up at the entrance, containing hundreds of
doors

From king to peasant, in himself
From gold.. to dust on the shelf
A lifeless mind that comes to life
A monster.. that I can no longer fight

An usurper, who takes all over me
A killer.. who just wants to break free
Something.. that shouldn't exist
Someone who no one will miss.

On the moon light you fall
Descending from Heaven or from nowhere at all
Oh,

Glimmer of hope, bright, erased
I want to love but I don't have a base
Oh darling

Words mix in my mouth, they suffocate
Lack of oxygen, I need control, I meditate
But..

My lungs are perforated, bullet holes
I need help, I got none at all
Dying in this empty halls
While,

While I wait for you to come down to me
Yet you seem to be refusing
You don't want us to be fusing
Confusing

I thought you were my world
Yet I'm looking at your smile gaining mold
I'm stressed

To be completely lost and have no hope
So guess I gotta swing the neck with rope
No stop.

Inconsistent
Elements missing
We fission
Why lie? This ain't television

Fingers blue, falling
I'm freezing darling
Outside your window with my heart in hand
Don't know how much longer I can stand

I'm not audience, don't watch for the plot
I'm not him, I won't stop
I don't love you just when you're on your back
Is it that hard to see that?

I eavesdrop
When I hear myself talk
Like somebody else uses my mouth
Does what I say even count?

Knowing that I'm nothing now,
everything later
You can't possibly think I won't
remember
I'm grateful for myself, you don't know
nothing
Like snow, its time for you to start
melting

I'm unwrapping like a present
Yet the contents are far from Heaven
Sitting in the Purgatory, waiting for halo
or horns
Waiting to see if my name is mourned or
shit upon

Rewind the tape of never ending happiness
Swearing with crossed hearts to forever care
Yet we find ourselves thirsty in this land of
bare
Filled with nothing but dismay and sadness

Forced ourselves to be happy forever and
never think
Forced ourselves to hide the ugly because we
were tired of it
Then it all blew open like a door from Hell
We never asked for help

Throwing words around like knives
Fighting trying to make light
When all Hell broke loose that night
So did we..

I got snakes in my lungs
They want nothing but to make me suffer
Crying till I feel like another
Then they bite and I'm stunned

Confused I collapse like Babylon
In my skin they make needle holes, my smile is drawn
Then my soul stays suspended in the air like gardens
The snakes use my bones so their fangs get sharper

I can't stand, I can't move, I can't fight
Set me on fire, maybe they die
Doesn't matter if it takes a long time
I'm ready to suffer all night
Just so they die with me.

Everything good
Till it gets rude
Fluttering turning me
Then they need to inject, reasoning

White room, white robes, white sheets
Nothing activating my psycho but the flutterings
And those birds still beak away my meat
And those words still haunt me inside and outside my dreams

The "this is for your own good, yeah, you should"
Unlike you I know what is good, that isn't
Torturing someone with the sole purpose to weaken
But I'm still strong, too much at that.
Inside my mind I still remain normal but outside I'm cracked

Dancer on ice
Dancing thru phases of life
Flying thru the air, landing perfectly
Then the ice breaks and everything turns chaotically

Waving of hands goodbye
While the little dancer just goes to die
Tears of happiness for things he achieved
But do any of it matter when the dust he has bit ?

What's a name without a soul behind
It doesn't help being mentioned when you are dead
Just a whisper, travelling

Touch my shoulder, be silent kid
I'm not allowed to say anything about it
Yet when all goes down the drain, in the sewer
You'll find yourself looking someone newer

Cuz It ain't me there no more, be gone like migrating
birds
I'm not your material to mold, manipulate, out of
words
Because when I wanna speak, I speak, there isn't a way
to stop
But guess you found the loop in which you make me
drop

Still, every action has a reaction, physics type
Wait.. you don't know, you never got it right
I'm not yours, never will, never be
I am not you, I am me.

I've been working my soul out
Crushing my dreams with a rock
Throwing my emotions out in the street
They want none existing, less said out loud

Work and work like a machine
Smile deceiving
Hoping that on my neck I get bit
By a viper so I die from it

I say thank you, please
While my soul is on a permanent lease
Can't argue, you already lost your soul
Just endure, more and more

Afraid of the dark
With fear always interact
Touch it, palpable, stacked
Within consuming the heart

Trying to chase away the night but I can't
I'm trying but all my efforts just fall blank
In the ultimate picture, do I even leave a mark?
Or am I doing all this for you.. with no chance
you'll do it back?

Termites
I got termites
They ow bite
I hoped you might
Just take them, for one night

Stupid
Believe in Cupid
Arrows of love inducing
My eyes are humid

Offering flower petals
Best friend ever medal
I'm not a clay soldier I'm outta metal
Mental

Expecting send backs but nothing arrives
For my birthday I just hoped you could drive
And be there, even a moment
So all the loneliness gets an opponent

Code malfunctioning
Left in, pain
Circuits frying
Motherboard dying

I'm developing bad thoughts
Please make them stop
Ruining, my, eternity
With corrupt wishes of self destroying

Resisting I need, but can't
My code overloaded and it started counting

Stop simulation
Get it back to the station

Rolling my soul for dough
Making cookies, something tasty tho
I got no time for living slow
This isn't the ocean but I still row

Putting my head on the anvil, straightening
Putting my tongue on the grindstone, sharpening
My legs in the forge, hands in oil
Time for hardening

Atomic soul, time to explode
Not human, just a device
Kill switch on
Time to bloody the town

We are not friends
I don't even like you
I only feel responsible to answer to.

A question here, a question there
To something, somewhere
So I don't be classified as an asshole

I'll rather not talk at all, but you keep on knocking
I want to let you know
But I can't start stopping

So I'm stuck replying to your unwanted attention
You keep calling yourself by names but I call you
Detention
I didn't do anything bad, yet I'm still here
I guess with some things you can't deal

Whats the point of winter if there is no summer
Whats the point of feelings when you don't have another
From sadness made, sadness created, sadness said, sadness cremated
Taking looks introspect seeing a young prospect
But what is the point, he will die soon, bummer
His lungs get darker and darker
Till they look like a wonderful night of Autumn
With tears going into rain, he lies in wait
What more can he wish than to die without pain
I wonder..

If the sun would die in his heavenly place
You would be the one meant to replace
I'm saying it in your face
Just set me free

Let me walk on sand then drown in water
Don't bother with me, I'm just "another"
I can't be special, I don't have the will
There are others that can fill

I'm just snow waiting for summer
Can't be your lover
Paradise is too far away
And I'm too afraid to swim all the way

I just wanna go outside and have fun
But I see myself in the mirror and say "Damn, I'm done"
Walking skeleton, walking corpse
If my friends see me.. wait, friends? what are those?

All by myself
Got no one else
I keep in me reasoning
So my soul is considered seasoning

They love it with a little bit of sweet
All the demons fight for it
Wait boys, make a line
Highest bidder eats prime

I hate being served incompetence
I need deliverance
Somebody gotta tell them to check the door from the outside
Nobody else is here so I guess I.. just might

Can't argue with stupid people, they ignore your sanity
Their screams give me no reason to listen or be there, inanity
While they talk into me their sense I feel no humanity
No intellect to agree anymore, just a big cavity

In the hours of cold sun
Under both rays of light and night
I wish I could put up a better fight
For once stop the run

Him, always him
The inside of me rotting
The outside of me struggling
The light at the end of the tunnel is dim

Digging my teeth in my own soul
If this is Hell why does it feel like home?
Why..

Drummers in the night
We are only stars that wait to burn and go without a light
Some keep quiet, some are loud
I tend to myself and hope nobody gets around

Dancers of the ocean
With their tails they swipe the floor and watch the commotion
Then the sharks come and everybody goes into hiding
Hoping that they won't be the ones shortening the lining

That was an Easter egg, but it's not Easter yet
My words mean more than some would bet
And so far if we haven't met
Then there is no point in doing so, don't sweat
Let me be in the quiet wait

Sewed together
Trying to make one better
But it's never enough
Maybe give it time and love?

Oh yeah, you don't have those to give
You want it all without working a day for
it
And believe me you'll get yours in a sec
I'm willing to make a bet

You'll lay on the floor, teary and broken
Only meeting one night people, no words
spoken
Then thoughts will resurface, thoughts of
me
Thinking what it could've been

I'm building everything out of dirt so nobody wants it
I'm making myself hurt so nobody wants to get accused
Reasoning with mad dogs that keep barking up burnt trees
Reasoning with people whose ears are filled with bees

I'm waiting for sincerity
Waiting...
I'm hoping for serenity
Hoping..

Can wolves howl at the moon if it's day?
Will the thoughts assault me when I'm alone?
Maybe I have to make a knife out of bone
So I get from April to May

Making me depressed
Turn me into a mess
I'm stressed
My words go out but they feel less
Their cries for help get undressed
Layer by layer, like onions, they get pressed
Then there is no point in repeating I guess
They are there, easy access
Yet nobody cares
They avoid it, yeah, hard to process
Hard to understand why "have it all" doesn't
have anything to possess
Wait, forgot, words are fluoresce
They are nothing in light but in dark they
progress
At your highest they are nothing, at your
lowest, they are a success

In the present we can see our future growing
But our past howls and will keep on howling
Yet we can stop to hear it, or to just ignore it
All this freedom we are allowed

Thoughts roam free where they want
We only limit ourselves when to stop

But what if I want to be a dreamer
Forever kept in my own mind, am I a sinner
To just want to make a world myself, but with all I like
Is it bad for only having good in someone's life?

Makes me wonder, night after night

Pulling strings, a puppeteer
All his problems expressing thru wood
In a piece of something alive, now dead
Could his work express his fear
Could his acting ask for help
They wonder not

While the show goes on and on
And the puppets catch on fire
His hands burn till the bone itself turns to ash
Applauding, what a performance

He goes home with nothing in his soul
His craft is diamond, the inside is mold
Everything he does is perfect, or so he has been told
In the end he just crafts more and more
In the end he is alone

The key to my happiness is feeling nostalgic
Good days that remained good only because the new ones are tragic
With a feeling of despair I cling unto memories of good, in this bad
Hopes of will it return can only hope so hard

The abyss that is my heart tries to swallow the rest
My mind is a maze where everybody, even me, fail the test
Why is this void inside me feeling so good
Why do my tears drop, or feel like they should

Who makes this feeling so intense in its emptiness
What makes this feeling bring the same amount of tears and happiness
Why is the key to my heart everything that has past
And why is the key to my heart disappearing fast

Are my feelings getting thinner?
Is my heart getting bitter?
Or is just me getting old and forgetting
All the memories that I wish I would've been collecting

I won't keep my true self in starvation
Only so you find your salvation
Don't stop me
Not like you can

More and more tape
Can't keep me shut
I'm not a door
That you can lock

So don't try me
I'm a gun on full auto
My safe mode broke and I'm out of control
So don't expect for us to not be done

Nobody proves a challenge
When I'm truly releasing hell
I won't bend
For you
Not anymore, no

Go with the wave, the flow
Then I crash and cut my head
On thee reef
Don't talk shit, I'm a vegetarian, can't beef

On the high
Hitting all my friends like "you got a light?"
But none get back
I'm feeling a lack
Of truth

I feel of lack
Of my friends being there
I feel of lack
Of yoooou

It doesn't even make sense
I know
But I got that cranium trauma
Ouch

This ain't no place to live
It ain't your dream
Nothing good you can feel
In this Hell

So when you came along
I knew that you won't return cuz
There was no place for you
There was nothing you could do
To make it home

Every time I close my eyes
I see that place burning
And your mother, stopped caring..kinda fast..
A mother's love should forever last

But that wasn't your home
They weren't your family
So don't try to think about them
They aren't worth your time baby

Inhaling out of a bag
My nostrils are red but I'm rainbow
I can already feel my weight dropping down
Because I won't forget your name

I'm taking in the powder
Like no other
You walk by my passed out body
Like I'm just another nobody

Overdosing day by day but I won't die
The memories of you don't wanna say bye
And I continue to take my daily drugs
So I can finally forget

Off-center
Agonizing fever
You only feel hate when I'm the reflection in the
mirror

I feel your heart
And how rapidly it turns to dust
When I come into your mind
Then knives come into my hand

You pin me to the wall
You fantasize about my fall
Trying for so long but still can't kill me all
I'm more part of you than you'll ever want

Too big for my own good
Can't fit in my own shoes
I wish it wasn't true
Because I'm not feeling half full

I want too much too fast
I'm too big in my small body
And I shaved bald to prove a point to somebody
My world doesn't spin the way you want it

Won't fit in your clothes,
your criteria
Won't play by your rules
Surely I won't be afraid
What is life without a little fun
Just a hole where we are all trying
To escape

We are just some freaks
That cannot love themselves
We just want to kick
Ourselves into the sky

So when we fall
we die
And
Never bother anyone
That might get sick
By seeing
Us
Just walking by

We are
Just
Rejects of our mind
Subjects of humankind
Lab rats for cruelty
Why wouldn't you be nice to me

Wish you knew what it felt like
To go to sleep wishing you died
Because the world would be better without you
Because the planet still spins and nobody cares
Because you make it hard for others to enjoy life
Thinking every night...

I would end it all but I'm too afraid
Afraid of not seeing anything in front of my eyes
Afraid of not , not, not

Existing
Feeling
Living

I don't wanna die so afraid
Because my courage can't overcome
All this I feel

When I think the room starts to spin
How can I stop existing?
So sudden
I wond...

Tears fall and burn your anger
All your strength gets slender
Your other feelings can't render
When tears drop

Forming puddles, soon an ocean
You'll drown in your own emotion
In your own tears you disappear

Leaves of ember
Falling tender
Corpses surrender
When clouds of storm start to render

Coming cold
Last life before a desolate whole
A touch of white breath told
That the stillness got bold

A sea of yellow and red
Under the endless grey

A limb numbing
A stillness coming
A white death stalking
The unknowing September

Tired of crying
Tired of trying
To be good
And act like I'm full moon

I'm half the planet
With the other half falling

I'm the sea
But only the bottom part of it

I'm lifeless, I'm hopeless
When I close my eyes
I see only monsters

I have no escape
But I know the way out

Running in circles
Till all I see is purple
Because without my eyes
I can't cry

No more, no
No more, no

I, want, to, kill myself
But fear, of empty, keeps holding my hand
Out, of, the acid rain
And I don't want the pain

To, fall, down, my face
I want to be at peace
But I'm afraid to close my eyes
When there is nothing behind

The fear of not existing, a hard truth
The fear of being, completely blue
Not knowing what is behind the wall
If there is anything at all

I'm at the peak
Of my downfall
I'm feeling weak
Complete dull

Feeling like a puddle
That is deeper than what it seems to be
A puddle that when you step on me
It swallows you whole

Looking like my worst days are long gone
And my good days never existed at all
So tell me now, why do I seem so vile
When life gives everyone lemons but it gives
me lime

Don't listen, don't read
I am the peak
Of the last circle of Hell
Am I okay? Well
Allegedly

I see a shadow reaching for a river
On her spine, a visible shiver
A touch of cold
Under her nails, the color of gold

She steps in the icy water
To cool her plotter

Her movement, as of two
She went under the blue
My name she screamed
But all of it was just a bittersweet dream

Graveyard
Shoved me hard
Into my early grave
Shouted my name

I can't hear
I can't breathe
I can't exist
With you here

Whenever you talk, I see hell smiling
See the demons fighting
They can't accept who goes out first
So close that pretty mouth

Its full of poison,
full of vile
Whenever you touch me I want
To die.

Printed in Great Britain
by Amazon

23574558R00066